Wendy Cope was born in Erith, Kent. After university she worked for fifteen years as a primary school teacher in London. Her first collection of poems, *Making Cocoa for Kingsley Amis*, was published in 1986. In 1987 she received a Cholmondeley Award for poetry, and in 1995 the American Academy of Arts and Letters Michael Braude Award for light verse. *Two Cures for Love: Selected Poems 1976–2006* was published in 2008.

Further praise for *Family Values*:

'Wendy Cope is as wittily subversive and honest as ever . . . love and compassionate humour fill this collection.' Sarah Wardle, *Guardian*

'Wonderful . . . Cope, like all the best poets, has the ability to twist the mundane and workaday into something new and enchanting. This book is full of bittersweet reflections on childhood, love and getting older. It offers consolation and hope to anyone who finds that they don't feel as old on the inside as they look.' Daisy Goodwin, *Sunday Times*

'Here is a poet in her prime and in command of her own delightful, deceptively demanding idiom.' Alan Taylor, *Herald*

'[Cope] has moments which are exquisite. The great quality of her poetry is that it is true.' Charles Moore, *Sunday Telegraph*

'*Family Values* is a highly enjoyable collection, combining approachability and formal ease with deeply felt emotion . . . Cope is one of those rare things: a popular and successful poet. This book will only increase that reputation.' Bookgeeks.co.uk

---

by the same author

MAKING COCOA FOR KINGSLEY AMIS
THE RIVER GIRL
SERIOUS CONCERNS
IF I DON'T KNOW
TWO CURES FOR LOVE: Selected Poems 1979–2006

for children
TWIDDLING YOUR THUMBS
GOING FOR A DRIVE

as editor
THE FUNNY SIDE: 101 Funny Poems
THE FABER BOOK OF BEDTIME STORIES
IS THAT THE NEW MOON?
THE ORCHARD BOOK OF FUNNY POEMS
HEAVEN ON EARTH: 101 Happy Poems
GEORGE HERBERT: A Selection

WENDY COPE

Family Values

faber and faber

First published in 2011
by Faber and Faber Ltd
Bloomsbury House
74–77 Great Russell Street
London WC1B 3DA

This paperback edition first published in 2012
Typeset by Faber and Faber Ltd
Printed in England by CPI Group (UK) Ltd, Croydon

A CIP record for this book
is available from the British Library

ISBN 978-0-571-28062-9

Acknowledgements

Acumen, Areté, Ariel, BBC Radio 3 and Radio 4, *Cadenza, Daily Telegraph, Dark Horse, Evansville Review* (USA), *Inside Out, Magma, Measure* (USA), *New Statesman, The Observer, Poetry* (USA), *Poetry Review, The Spectator, Tatler, The Times, Times Literary Supplement.*

Howard Goodall's setting of 'Spared' can be heard on the CD *Eternal Light* (EMI Classics); the score is published by Faber Music. The score of 'The Audience' by Roxanna Panufnik is published by Edition Peters.

Six of the poems in this book also appear in *Two Cures for Love: Selected Poems 1979–2006.* The first part of 'Differences of Opinion' ('He Tells Her') is in *If I Don't Know* (2001).

Contents

Family Values

A Christmas Song

Why is the baby crying
On this, his special day,
When we have brought him lovely gifts
And laid them on the hay?

He's crying for the people
Who greet this day with dread
Because somebody dear to them
Is far away or dead,

For all the men and women
Whose love affairs went wrong,
Who try their best at merriment
When Christmas comes along,

For separated parents
Whose turn it is to grieve
While children hang their stockings up
Elsewhere on Christmas Eve,

For everyone whose burden,
Carried through the year,
Is heavier at Christmastime,
The season of good cheer.

That's why the baby's crying
There in the cattle stall:
He's crying for those people.
He's crying for them all.

Christmas Ornaments

The mice attacked the Holy Family –
The one I bought in Prague, made out of straw.
By Christmas, Joseph was an amputee
And Mary and the baby were no more.
But I have other treasures to display –
Two perching birds, a Santa Claus, a clown,
A rooster from the church in Santa Fé,
A little harp and drum, a shoe, a crown –
Collected in the years I've lived with you,
The years of warmth and love and Christmas trees,
And someone to come home to, someone who
Can share what I bring back from overseas
And sometimes travel with me. Darling, look –
Our moon from Paris, glittering on its hook.

Cathedral Carol Service

Those of us who are not important enough
To have places reserved for us,
And who turned up too late to get a seat at all,
Stand in the nave aisles, or perch on stone ledges.

We shiver in the draught from the west door.
We cannot see the choir, the altar or the candles.
We can barely see the words on our service sheets.

But we can hear the music. And we can sing
For the baby whose parents were not important enough
To have a place reserved for them,
And who turned up too late to get a room at all.

O Come, All Ye Faithful

Born the King of Angels –
That's the bit drives music teachers
Round the bend. 'It's An-gels.
Two notes. Not A-an-gels.'
I've fought some battles
With that extra note
And still get wound up every Christmas.

Daddy had a different problem
With the same hymn.
Sing all ye citizens
Of Heaven above.
'Heaven', he asserted,
'Is not a city.
It should be *denizens*.'

And that was what he sang.
It wasn't too embarrassing
But I can't sing the verse
Without remembering. In recent years
I have paid tribute to his memory
By singing, rather quietly,
'Denizens of Heaven above.'

Differences of Opinion

1 *He Tells Her*

He tells her that the earth is flat –
He knows the facts, and that is that.
In altercations fierce and long
She tries her best to prove him wrong.
But he has learned to argue well.
He calls her arguments unsound
And often asks her not to yell.
She cannot win. He stands his ground.

The planet goes on being round.

2 *Your Mother Knows*

Your mother *knows* the earth's a plane
And, challenged, sheds a martyr's tear.
God give her strength to bear this pain –
A child who says the world's a sphere!

Challenged, she sheds a martyr's tear.
It's bad to make your mother cry
By telling her the world's a sphere.
It's very bad to tell a lie.

It's bad to make your mother cry.
It's bad to think your mother odd.
It's very bad to tell a lie.
All this has been ordained by God.

It's bad to think your mother odd.
The world is round. That's also true.
All this has been ordained by God.
It's hard to see what you can do.

The world is round. That *must* be true.
She's praying, hoping you will change.
It's hard to see what you can do.
Already people find you strange.

She's praying, hoping you will change.
You're difficult. You don't fit in.
Already people find you strange.
You know your anger is a sin.

You're difficult. You don't fit in.
God give her strength to bear this pain.
You know your anger is a sin.
Your mother knows the earth's a plane.

Sunday Morning

Sunday morning. Things get tense.
Will I go along
To church with Mummy or stay home,
Depressed and in the wrong?

It's a communion service
And I cannot go up,
A doubter and a sinner,
To take the silver cup.

I'll get my coat and come with you
As long as you don't mind
If, when you go up to the front,
I choose to stay behind.

But that is not acceptable.
She says it will not do.
If you don't take communion,
What will they think of you?

It's better if you stay at home,
She tells me angrily,
Which means another ruined day
For Mummy and for me.

You're Not Allowed

You're not allowed to wonder if it's true:
She loves you very much. She tells you so.
She is the one who knows what's best for you.
She tells you what to do and where to go.

She loves you very much. She tells you so.
That's why she's sending you to boarding school.
She tells you what to do and where to go
And there is no appeal against her rule.

And now she's sending you to boarding school.
She'll be upset if you are cross and sad.
And there is no appeal against this rule:
If Mummy is upset, you must be bad.

Her children often make her cross and sad
And then she cries. She cries and sulks all day.
If Mummy is upset, you must be bad.
It's no good saying sorry. You must pay.

You watch her cry. She cries and sulks all day.
You'd make your mother happy, if you could.
It's no use saying sorry. You must pay.
Things will get better, if you're very good.

You'd make your mother happy, if you could.
She is the one who knows what's best for you.
Things will get better, if you're very good.
You're not allowed to wonder if it's true.

Daily Help

In memory of Margaret Arnold 1900–91

I

You seem so small
now you are old
and I am not a child.
Your hair is yellow-white,
your eyes have paled

to the colour of the sea
on summer evenings
and the hands
that cleaned our house for years
are puffed and painful.

You don't need us now –
your children care for you;
their grandchildren
demand your company
as eagerly as we did.

Yet that huge photograph
of us remains in place.
And when I visit you
you say, 'I can't help
loving you, you know.'

Others taught us to be prudent,
thrifty, fold our serviettes –
all those important lessons.
We hug. Tears disarrange
my manners as I leave.

2

If Mrs Arnold yelled at Marian
To come and put her pyjamas away,
Marian just ran upstairs and did it.
No argument. No tears.
And she was instantly forgiven.
Mrs Arnold didn't sulk all day
If you did something wrong.

It wasn't just that she was nicer
Than Mummy. She radiated love
Like a little walking sun
And children loved her back.

We heard a lot about her grandsons,
Who were our age. Later on
I learned she'd had a daughter
Who had died in childhood
And I saw a photograph – a girl
With curly hair like mine.

When we'd moved away
She was a star turn as a dinner-lady
In her local school. But she missed us.

Before I went to boarding school
When I was seven, I asked her
To kiss my teddy bear
Because he was coming with me
And the kiss would come too.
In the darkness of the dormitory
I held his cheek to mine
And knew that Mrs Arnold
Was kissing me goodnight.

Boarders

I

Boarders are better than daygirls.
We never questioned that belief.

We were tough. We could survive
Without our mummies and our daddies,

Not like feeble daygirls.
'Feeble' was our worst insult.

Secretly I knew I was feeble
And lived in fear of being teased.

'Teasing' was our word for bullying.
The bossy girls picked out the victims,

Sometimes turning on one of their own.
Mostly it was verbal;

Now and then a cry went up,
'Chase for Trudy Tipple!'

The girl took flight. The mob
Pursued its human quarry.

I didn't join in. I like to think
It wasn't just because I couldn't run.

Once there was a special party:
Every boarder had to invite a daygirl.

My choice was Susan Bird,
A gentle girl. I liked her face.

I felt I was doing her an honour.
I was willing to be her friend.

But nothing came of it.
Even though I was a boarder

And she a mere daygirl,
She didn't jump at the chance.

I wasn't teased much. The worst time
Was in my first year

Because some older girls decided
That I used too many long words.

I soon learned not to.
Look at how I write.

Omo

One cold day, emerging
From the cloakroom,
Wrapped up in a hooded coat
And gloves and boots,
She announced 'I'm an Omo!'

When I'd stopped laughing
I told her the word was 'Eskimo'
But after that I called her 'Omo'
And it caught on. It was affectionate.
She never complained.

They called me 'Copper'
Because it was a bit like Cope.
We were a pair: Copper and Omo.
We sat together, played together,
And the bullies left us alone.

I still love Omo.
These days I use her real name
But I don't dare to mention it.
She hides from cameras. And now
I've gone and put her in a poem.

The Women's Merchant Navy

Mummy's cousin Evelyn,
Who was more like a sister to her,
Married an officer
In the Merchant Navy. Eddie Snaith.

He served on convoys
All through World War II.
Dangerous work.
His whereabouts were always secret.

He had his master's ticket.
Early in the fifties he got a ship.
A ship's captain!
I was very proud of him.

I learned that you could join
The Royal Navy, if you were a woman,
And be a Wren. I asked
About the Women's Merchant Navy.

There wasn't one,
Which seemed all wrong to me.
I decided I would found it
When I grew up.

It lasted quite a long time,
That ambition. When I was eleven
I went for an interview
At a new school.

'What do you want to do
When you grow up?'
The headmistress asked.
'Found the Women's Merchant Navy.'

She looked at my mother,
Who explained about Uncle Eddie.
I had a strong suspicion
That both of them thought it was funny.

The Africans

Visitors from Africa!
I must have been three or four
When I was told they were coming.

I knew about Africans from picture books.
They had black skin. They wore grass skirts
And beads. They danced around with spears.
I was excited and a bit scared.

When the day arrived
I stood in the back garden,
Looking through a wrought-iron gate
At the path to the front door.

And there they were, the Africans,
But they were white. Their clothes
Were just like ours.

I don't know if I hid my disappointment.
Was I good?
The rest of the day is lost.

But I can see them now,
Their many-coloured beads,
Their black skins shining,

Grass skirts rustling,
As they enter our suburban garden
And walk towards the house.

Uncle Bill

Mummy's working-class relations
Didn't get invited to dinner or tea
But Uncle Bill dropped in
From time to time, to see Nanna
Because she was his sister.
'Hello Uncle Bill,' we'd say
As he passed through the hall
On his way to the kitchen
Or Nanna's room.
He didn't stay long. When he left
We said goodbye. And that
Was all we ever saw of Uncle Bill.

Except that sometimes we'd be on a bus –
You got on at the back
And didn't see the driver –
And, even though we'd pinged to get off,
It went on past our stop
Until it reached our house.
We jumped off, my sister and I,
And ran along to the driver's cab.
'Uncle Bill! Uncle Bill!'
He waved back and drove away.

Brahms Cradle Song

I've heard it on the radio
Twice in two days –
In an item about sleep
And in *Cider with Rosie*,
When Laurie plays it on the violin,
Much too fast, like a jig.

My mother used to sing it to me
At bedtime. I liked the tune
And the words: roses,
Silvery light, God
Watching over us
Until it's time to wake up.

She read me *Black Beauty*.
She made me learn the piano.
She taught me to swim,
Despite Daddy's fear of the water,
And, after the accident
In the instructor's car, to drive.

For all that, I am grateful.
As for the rest, I can begin
To imagine forgiving her
When I am reminded
Of a young woman singing
About roses asleep in the dew.

Greydawn

We used it every day
When I was growing up.
The name stamped on the back
Is *Greydawn* – all one word.
It isn't grey. It's blue.

I made this point quite often.
'Why do they call it grey?'
The grown-ups didn't know
And tired of the question.
I still wonder.

There are three plates left –
Medium-sized, pudding plates.
All the rest – dinner and cheese plates,
Soup bowls – have disappeared,
Like the people who used them.

Mummy, Daddy, Nanna,
Sitting round the dining-room table.
And I have spun through the air
Into the future, all by myself,
With three of our blue plates.

At Stafford Services

*. . . places of transit where we are aware
of a particular kind of alienated poetry.*
— ALAIN DE BOTTON

In the Wimpy Bar at Stafford services
I ask for ketchup. The girl gives me a sachet.
She seems nice, so I mention the red plastic tomatoes
That used to be on every table in the old days.
She has never heard of them. She thinks
Ketchup on the tables is a good idea.

The red plastic tomatoes, the formica tables
In the Wimpy Bar by Barnehurst bus depot
Where I went, aged thirteen, to smoke,
Drink coffee and feel sophisticated.
It was all so modern, so American, so young,
And a safe haven from parents.

Fifty years on I'm sitting in another one,
Drinking coffee and not smoking.
As the light fades the glass walls turn into mirrors,
Lending the place an air of glamour. I like it here.
I could be in an Edward Hopper painting,
A woman travelling alone on business.

No-one knows anything about me. Perhaps
I'm a high-powered executive with a BMW
Outside in the car park. Or some kind of artist,
A poet, maybe, scribbling in her notebook.
Dreams in a Wimpy. I finish my coffee,
Find my keys, and walk out of the picture.

At the Poetry Conference

Melancholy's grape: today I've bitten it.
I'm sad because you live so far away.
I need to write a poem but I've written it
Already: 1989, LA.

Here we are again and I am crying.
Nothing has changed except that we are old.
We will be far apart when we are dying.
One will go. The other will be told

By phone or email and it will be over.
The survivor will sit down and weep
And write a poem mourning the ex-lover
And have a drink or two and go to sleep.

That will be that. You see I'm alternating
Two kinds of rhyme, the way you recommend.
I trust you'll give these lines a Grade A rating
And that, of course, will cheer me up no end.

The Health Scare

I'm living with Uncertainty and Fear.
I need to say their names and make them rhyme.
Two monsters. I can't make them disappear.
I'm living with Uncertainty and Fear.
Though abstract nouns are not a good idea,
And abstract nouns with capitals, a crime,
I'm living with Uncertainty and Fear.
It helps to say their names and make them rhyme.

Sixty-one

Sixty-one and on a diet.
Will I end up thin or fat
When my heart and brain go quiet?
Sixty-one and on a diet
Yet again. My hopes run riot:
Better life, new start – all that.
Sixty-one and on a diet.
Will I end up thin or fat?

Keep Saying This

Keep saying this and don't forget:
Although you think you're very old,
The party isn't over yet.

You lie awake at night beset
By dread of being dead and cold.
Keep saying this and don't forget:

It doesn't help at all to fret
About what cannot be controlled.
The party isn't over yet.

Although your nature wasn't set
In a serene or fearless mould,
Keep saying this and don't forget:

In ten years time you may regret
Surrendering to gloom. Be bold.
The party isn't over yet.

No point in living if you let
Your terror of the end take hold.
Keep saying this and don't forget
The party isn't over yet.

Once I'm Dead

Once I'm dead, I won't mind being dead.
Why worry? I don't want to say goodbye
To everything, to me – the voice that said
'Once I'm dead, I won't mind being dead',
The words are comforting. But still I dread
The day that we must part, myself and I.
The voice may still be heard when I am dead
But not by me. I will have said goodbye.

My Funeral

I hope I can trust you, friends, not to use our relationship
As an excuse for an unsolicited ego-trip.
I have seen enough of them at funerals and they make
    me cross.
At this one, though deceased, I aim to be the boss.
If you are asked to talk about me for five minutes, please
    do not go on for eight.
There is a strict timetable at the crematorium and nobody
    wants to be late.
If invited to read a poem, just read the bloody poem.
    If requested
To sing a song, just sing it, as suggested,
And don't say anything. Though I will not be there,
Glancing pointedly at my watch and fixing the speaker
    with a malevolent stare,
Remember that this was how I always reacted
When I felt that anybody's speech, sermon or poetry reading
    was becoming too protracted.
Yes, I was impatient and intolerant, and not always polite
And if there aren't many people at my funeral, it will
    serve me right.

Seeing You

Seeing you will make me sad.
I want to do it anyway.
We can't relive the times we had –
Seeing you will make me sad.
Perhaps it's wrong. Perhaps it's mad,
But we will both be dead one day.
Seeing you will make me sad.
I have to do it anyway.

Macedonia 1987

A little crowd had gathered in the square.
We read our poems and they were polite.
Then there was dinner in the open air
Outside the castle. A warm summer night.
The local bigwigs lit up their cigars
And asked us for a song, and, straight away,
You stood. I see you underneath the stars.
I hear your voice. I hear it to this day.
I too can sing but I am English, so,
Although I wanted to, I didn't dare.
And still, though that was twenty years ago,
A male voice singing German takes me there.
Bach and Schubert won't let me forget
That evening, five days after we first met.

Dutch Portraits

To find myself in tears is a surprise –
Paintings don't often get to me like this:
These faces with their vulnerable eyes
And lips so soft that they invite a kiss;
The long-haired husband, gazing at his bride
With evident desire, his hand around
Her wrist, six years before she died –
Both so alive and so long underground.
And here's a husband who resembles you
When you were plump and bearded. It's too much.
He looks so happy and his wife does too,
Still smiling, now they can no longer touch.
Someone will read our story, by and by.
Perhaps they'll feel like this. Perhaps they'll cry.

Haiku

A perfect white wine
is sharp, sweet and cold as this:
birdsong in winter.

April

The birds are singing loudly overhead,
As if to celebrate the April weather.
I want to stay in this lovely world forever
And be with you, my love, and share your bed.

I don't believe I'll see you when we're dead.
I don't believe we'll meet and be together.
The birds are singing loudly overhead.
I want to stay in this lovely world forever.

The Month of May

O! the month of May, the merry month of May ...
    – THOMAS DEKKER (d. 1632)

The month of May, the merry month of May,
So long awaited, and so quickly past.
The winter's over, and it's time to play.

I saw a hundred shades of green today
And everything that Man made was outclassed.
The month of May, the merry month of May.

Now hello pink and white and farewell grey.
My spirits are no longer overcast.
The winter's over and it's time to play.

Sing 'Fa la la la la', I dare to say
(Tried being modern but it didn't last),
'The month of May, the merry month of May.'

I don't know how much longer I can stay.
The summers come, the summers go so fast,
And soon there will be no more time to play.

So *carpe diem*, gather buds, make hay.
The world is glorious. Compare, contrast
December with the merry month of May.
Now is the time, now is the time to play.

Lissadell

Last year we went to Lissadell.
The sun shone over Sligo Bay
And life was good and all was well.

The bear, the books, the dinner-bell,
An air of dignified decay.
Last year we went to Lissadell.

This year the owners had to sell –
It calls to mind a Chekhov play.
Once life was good and all was well.

The house is now an empty shell,
The contents auctioned, shipped away.
Last year we went to Lissadell

And found it magical. 'We fell
In love with it', we sometimes say
When life is good and all is well.

The light of evening. A gazelle.
It seemed unchanged since Yeats's day.
Last year we went to Lissadell
And life was good and all was well.

At Steep

We stumble down the sloping path
Clutching at trunks and branches, then
A few more steps, another tree,
Until at last we see the stone.

'That must be it.' There is no sign
On road or path to say it's there
But walkers pass this way and learn
Your name and find out who you were,

And pilgrims clutching leaflets come
From time to time, walk half a mile
To sit by your memorial
And keep you company awhile.

No. You're beyond all company.
Numbers and words inscribed on stone
Are all that's left of you where once
You felt the sun, the blessed rain.

Numbers and words inscribed on stone.
You're dead and gone and speaking still.
Your spirit lives; it brought us here.
You cannot know, and never will.

Note: Edward Thomas lived at Steep in Hampshire.
There is a memorial to him on a hillside outside the village.

A Villanelle for Hugo Williams

What can I say? I'd like to be polite
But have you ever *seen* a villanelle?
You ask me 'Have I got the rhyme-scheme right?'

Is that a joke? You're not a neophyte
Or some green-inker who can barely spell.
What can I say? I like to be polite.

No, not exactly, Hugo. No, not quite.
I trust this news won't plunge you into hell:
Your rhyme-scheme is some miles from being right.

What's going on? I know you're very bright.
You've won awards. You write supremely well.
What can I say? I like to be polite

And this is true: your books are a delight,
In prose, free verse and letters you excel.
You want my help with getting rhyme-schemes right.

You seem dead keen to master them, despite
Your puzzling inability to tell
Which bit goes where. These lines, if not polite,
Will be of use, I hope. The rhyme-scheme's right.

Two Ann(e)s

for Anne Harvey and Ann Thwaite
(who were at school together)

Anne with an e and Ann without
Were clever girls and good at spelling.
Their teachers couldn't catch them out –
Anne with an e and Ann without.
I hope that you are clear about
Which Ann(e) is which and won't need telling.
Anne with an e and Ann without –
Don't trifle with them. Watch your spelling.

Special Needs

Some pupils here have special needs
Which must be borne in mind.
We monitor them carefully,
In case they fall behind:
The dyslexic, the dyspraxic
And the disinclined.

Old Boys' Day

Row upon row of grey heads
In a chapel built for the young.
I picture them as rows of boys
Who knew, but didn't quite believe,
They would grow old and die.

Once I might have taken them
For sour-faced old buffers.
Now I see they are moved,
That I am not the only person
Who is close to tears.

Yes, there are smiles
Exchanged between friends
When they hear a well-remembered flourish
In the hymn accompaniment
But this is a sombre occasion.

After the service there are drinks,
Warm greetings, an outbreak
Of cheerfulness. It's like the party
After a funeral. And then goodbye –
Goodbye, old chap. Until next year.

Probably

If I'm not sure, I can't say yes.
You need an answer by today.
Probably. Unless. Unless

I've freaked from all the strain and stress,
They've come and carted me away.
If I'm not sure, I can't say yes.

If I'm alive, at this address,
I'll try to do it. I can say
Probably. Unless. Unless

I'm down with flu or in some mess
So dire that I can't work or play.
If I'm not sure, I can't say yes.

I cannot guarantee success.
I'll blow it, forfeiting the pay,
Probably. Unless. Unless

I ask for help in my distress.
Does someone hear me when I pray?
If I'm not sure, I can't say yes.
Probably. Unless. Unless.

Stars

The hotter the star, the bluer it shines.
The smaller the star, the longer it lives.
It shouldn't be hard to remember these lines
(The hotter the star, the bluer it shines).
You can search the night sky for meaningful signs,
Or study it just for the pleasure it gives.
The hotter the star, the bluer it shines.
The smaller the star, the longer it lives.

An Anniversary Poem

*Tenth anniversary of the ordination of the first women priests
in the Church of England in February 1994*

Good Christian men and women, let us raise a joyful shout:
The C of E is treating us as equals. Just about.

Sister, fetch the fatted calf, and we'll prepare a feast:
You can't become a bishop but you can become a priest.

The mountains skip like rams, the little hills like sheep.
    And why?
Our problem-solving miracle: a bishop who can fly.

Sing, dance, clap your hands, make merry and be glad:
Some men behave atrociously, but most are not too bad.

Bring out the tambourines, and let the trumpet sound:
These years have not been easy but, praise God, you're
    still around,

Brave, forgiving pioneers. May this be your reward:
To grow in strength and beauty in the service of the Lord.

But should there be a woman Primate while I'm still alive,
Oh, then we'll hear the valleys sing, and see the mountains jive.

*Note: 'Flying bishops' were appointed for the benefit of male clergy
who oppose the ordination of women and are therefore at odds
with their diocesan bishop.*

Spared

That Love is all there is,
Is all we know of Love . . .
− EMILY DICKINSON

It wasn't you, it wasn't me,
Up there, two thousand feet above
A New York street. We're safe and free,
A little while, to live and love,

Imagining what might have been −
The phone-call from the blazing tower,
A last farewell on the machine,
While someone sleeps another hour,

Or worse, perhaps, to say goodbye
And listen to each other's pain,
Send helpless love across the sky,
Knowing we'll never meet again,

Or jump together, hand in hand,
To certain death. Spared all of this
For now, how well I understand
That love is all, is all there is.

Another Valentine

Today we are obliged to be romantic
And think of yet another valentine.
We know the rules and we are both pedantic:
Today's the day we have to be romantic.
Our love is old and sure, not new and frantic.
You know I'm yours and I know you are mine.
And saying that has made me feel romantic,
My dearest love, my darling valentine.

from The Audience

Poems commissioned by the Endellion String Quartet

Prologue: The Performers

You set off in the morning with a little time to spare.
You should be fine. You should be nice and early getting there.
And everything is hunky-dory till you see a tail
Of traffic that is moving rather slower than a snail.
Ah well, you think, *the chances are I won't be stuck here long.*
This optimistic view turns out to be completely wrong.
And, several hours later, when you limp into the city
Where you need to be, you're fighting off a headache and
      self-pity.
And you know that at the tail end of this long and tiring day
You must sit down in a concert hall, take up your bow
      and play.

The venue sent a map but it's no effing use at all,
So you drive around and drive around until you want to bawl,
Then suddenly you notice that, by chance, you're driving past
Your destination. Turn around, and you've arrived at last.
And, yes, they have a car park but the entrance is behind
The building, round a corner, and it's rather hard to find.
But finally you're parked and you've unloaded all your stuff
And carried it inside. By now you've really had enough.
And you know that at the tail end of this long and tiring day
You must sit down in a concert hall, take up your bow
      and play.

49

And now there's a rehearsal, interrupted by the need
To get the lighting altered, so that you can see to read,
To fiddle with the music stands, to find some different chairs.
You're trying not to act like rather tender-headed bears.
Then you go off to the green room, which, although it
    doesn't smell,
Does not resemble in the least a luxury hotel.
You change your clothes and comb your hair and hope you
    look all right.
You'd like to have a drink but can't – it's no good getting tight.
For you know that at the tail end of this long and tiring day
You must sit down in the concert hall, take up your bow
    and play.

The auditorium is full, the instruments in tune.
You're feeling slightly nervous. Zero hour is very soon.
You're shepherded towards the wings and there you have
    to pause
Until it's time to enter and acknowledge the applause.
You hope you won't trip over as you walk towards your seat.
You hope you've done your zip up but it's too late to retreat.
The people in the audience are silent as they sit
And wait for something wonderful to happen. This is it.
You sit up straight and you forget your long and tiring day
As you focus on the music and take up your bow and play.

The Cougher

There's a tickle in your throat
And you've hardly heard a note
And you're wishing you were in some other place.
In this silent, listening crowd
You're the one who'll cough out loud,
And you know you're facing imminent disgrace.

Yes, right now you're in a pickle.
The unmanageable tickle
Is a torment, and it's threatening your poise.
Can you hold out any longer
As the urge to cough grows stronger?
Any moment you'll emit a mighty noise.

If this bloody piece were shorter,
If you had a glass of water,
It would help. But there is nothing you can do.
Oh, if only you could be
Safe at home with a CD,
In an armchair, free to cough the whole way through.

Do you hear a rallentando?
Does this mean the end's at hand? Oh,
What a mercy. Yes, they're really signing off.
They perform the closing bars
And you thank your lucky stars
And it's over. You have made it. You may cough.

The Traditionalist

I like a good tune with a regular beat
From the days before music went wrong –
An old-fashioned melody, catchy and sweet.
I like a good tune with a regular beat.
These modern composers, they can't write a song.
They don't get you tapping your feet.
I like a good tune with a regular beat
From the days before music went wrong.

The Radical

I've little patience with this kind of thing –
This trite, post-modern, easy listening.
I hoped for something far more challenging.
This isn't avant-garde enough.
It really isn't hard enough.
It isn't avant-garde enough for me.

The point is not to please the bourgeois ear.
The good composer is a pioneer
Whose music very few will want to hear.
This isn't cutting-edge enough.
It isn't off-the-ledge enough.
It isn't cutting-edge enough for me.

Art should disturb. It's not to make us glad.
It isn't to console us when we're sad.
It's to remind us that the world is bad.
This isn't agonised enough.
You're not antagonised enough.
It isn't agonised enough for me.

Repeat ad lib:
It really isn't hard enough.
It isn't avant-garde enough   *etc.*

The Critic

I hear it once and then I have to write
Six hundred words about it the same night,
Or early in the morning, and submit
A piece displaying polish, wisdom, wit.

It's hard to think of new and different ways
Of being negative or giving praise,
And when you've penned a decade of reviews
You're sick of all the adjectives you use.

Exquisite, brilliant, superb, first-rate.
Impressive, masterly, outstanding, great,
Inept, monotonous, indifferent, bad.
Atrocious, terrible, sub-standard, mad,

And so on. I work hard to make it just,
To be the kind of critic you can trust.
I do my very best. I send it in.
One day's exposure. Then it's in the bin.

First Date

SHE

I said I liked classical music.
It wasn't exactly a lie.
I hoped he would get the impression
That my brow was acceptably high.

I said I liked classical music.
I mentioned Vivaldi and Bach.
And he asked me along to this concert.
Here we are, sitting in the half-dark.

I was thrilled to be asked to the concert.
I couldn't decide what to wear.
I hope I look tastefully sexy.
I've done what I can with my hair.

Yes, I'm thrilled to be here at this concert.
I couldn't care less what they play
But I'm trying my hardest to listen
So I'll have something clever to say.

When I glance at his face it's a picture
Of rapt concentration. I see
He is totally into this music
And quite undistracted by me.

First Date

She said she liked classical music.
I implied I was keen on it too.
Though I don't often go to a concert,
It wasn't entirely untrue.

I looked for a suitable concert
And here we are, on our first date.
The traffic was dreadful this evening
And I arrived ten minutes late.

So we haven't had much time for talking
And I'm a bit nervous. I see
She is totally lost in the music
And quite undistracted by me.

In that dress she is very attractive –
The neckline can't fail to intrigue.
I mustn't appear too besotted.
Perhaps she is out of my league.

Where are we? I glance at the programme
But I've put my glasses away.
I'd better start paying attention
Or else I'll have nothing to say.

The Widow

I like this piece. I think you'd like it too.
We didn't very often disagree
Back in the days when I sat here with you
And knew that you were coming home with me.
This is the future. It arrived so fast.
When we were young it seemed so far away.
Our years together vanished like a day
At nightfall, sealed forever in the past.
I can't give up on music, just discard
The interest we shared because you died.
And so I come to concerts. But it's hard.
Tonight I'm doing well. I haven't cried.
My head aches. There's a tightness in my throat.
And you will never hear another note.

A Rehearsal

For Roxanna Panufnik and the Endellion String Quartet

How shall we play this? We have all got votes,
The six of us rehearsing here today.
Hang on a minute. Can I check my notes?
You want a B flat here? You're sure? OK.

Six of us rehearsing here today,
Composer, poet and a string quartet
(You want a creaky sound? Like this? OK),
And do we all have points to make? You bet.

Composer, poet and a string quartet –
The poet has a *rôle* as the narrator –
And do we all have points to make? You bet.
Too fast. Too loud. You need to come in later.

The poet has a *rôle* as the narrator.
Her lips are moving as she tries to count.
Bar 92. You need to come in later.
We have some little problems to surmount.

Her lips are moving as she tries to count.
The first performance is a week away.
We have some little problems to surmount.
It's going to be fine. That's what we say.

The first performance is a week away.
Now shall we play it through? We've all got votes.
It's going to be fine. That's what we say.
Hang on a minute. Can I check my notes?

from An ABC of the BBC

Poems commissioned by BBC Radio 4

The Archers and Adultery

I like *The Archers* only when it's got
Adulterous behaviour in the plot.
Just when it was becoming one long yawn
They gave us – yippee! – Brian and Siobhan.
I was delighted. I did not care tuppence
When smug, kept Jennifer got her comeuppance.

Then there was Ruth's flirtation. Would she do it
With Sam? Of course she wouldn't and I knew it.
I said it all along. I had no doubt.
She got to the hotel and bottled out.
So now she'll be a good, upstanding wife
('Oh, no!') six episodes a week for life.

She'll be like all the other Archers, who
Like nothing better than a family do,
With everyone together. Young and old
Content to be within the family fold,
With no-one wishing that they could avoid it,
And everybody saying they enjoyed it.

Yes, in *The Archers* family values reign.
The straying spouses all come back again.
Sam disappeared and poor Siobhan is dead
And we get problems with the cows instead.
I listen sometimes, doing random checks,
So I'll know when there's more illicit sex.

Digital and Interactive

for Julian May

The producer wants me to write about digital and interactive.
I have tried but I do not find these subjects attractive.
There is a gap and this attempt to bridge it'll
Be all there is on interactive or on digital.

Football

A most delightful programme
Goes out on Saturday
When football fans ring Radio 5,
All keen to have their say.

Caller after caller
Whose team is doing badly
Will tell us what the problem is,
More angrily than sadly.

There are two explanations
For failure, as a rule:
The referee's a villain or
The manager's a fool.

The Radio 5 presenter
Is rational and calm,
Defending refs against the men
Who want to do them harm,

Who want them to be punished
For their defective vision –
Dismissed, disgraced and disembowelled
For every bad decision.

The righteous rage! The passion!
I'm not a football fan
But this is first-rate comedy.
I listen when I can.

The Middle Classes

When BBC top brasses
Play games with Radio Four,
The angry middle classes
Rise up and say 'No more!'

'Don't meddle with our programmes,
Don't change a thing because
We are your faithful listeners.
We liked it as it was.'

The weeks go by. We settle,
Recover from the shock
Of learning that *The Archers*
Is now at two o'clock,

And we adjust our habits.
Astonishingly soon,
We don't recall that *Woman's Hour*
Was in the afternoon.

But if some new controller
Starts changing things again
You can be sure we'll have our say,
Protest with voice and pen.

And so the decade passes,
As decades did of yore.
Long live the middle classes
And long live Radio Four.

Quizzes

I'm always glad when there's a quiz
To make my little brain cells fizz.
I get to show off all my wealth
Of general knowledge to myself.

But, any time I'm asked to go
And take part on the radio,
I straight away decline the chance
To show off all my ignorance.

Unbearable
or *Things that make me switch the radio off*

Talk of scary medical conditions,
Clichés from the mouths of politicians,

Interviewers whose self-righteous tone
Suggests they have the right to cast a stone,

Too much aggression early in the day
(Just press a switch and it will go away),

Reporters whose command of English grammar
Deserves a beta minus or a gamma,

Comedians making unkind jokes about
A person's looks (no thank you; count me out),

Actors being actorish, and, worse,
The voice of Dylan Thomas reading verse.

X-rated

for Horatio Clare

If someone wants to use a naughty word
The rule is that is has to be referred
To someone higher up, who must decide
If saying the said word is justified.

Some listeners, of course, will have a fit
If anyone's permitted to say it
And lots of people will be horror-struck
To hear the BBC broadcasting muck.

So there's a person in an office who
Considers all those words for me and you.
The same old words come back and back again –
She probably employs them now and then.

Closedown

for Alice Arnold

An almost empty building:
Someone, all alone,
Reads the shipping forecast
To a microphone.

Listeners in bedrooms,
Listeners at sea,
Thousands of them, hear her
Speak invisibly,

Hear her through the darkness,
Hear her say goodnight,
Picture her alone there,
Switching off the light.

Is it really like that?
I asked if I could go
And be with the announcer
In the studio.

And, yes, it's really like that.
Someone, all alone,
Reads the shipping forecast
To a microphone,

Speaks into the darkness,
Says a last goodnight,
Plays the national anthem,
Switches off the light.